Managing Employees

Young Adult Library of
Small Business and Finance

Building a Business in the Virtual World

Business & Ethics

Business & the Government: Law and Taxes

Business Funding & Finances

Keeping Your Business Organized:
Time Management & Workflow

Managing Employees

Marketing Your Business

Starting a Business: Creating a Plan

Understanding Business Math & Budgets

What Does It Mean to Be an Entrepreneur?

Young Adult Library of Small Business and Finance

Managing Employees

Helen Thompson

Mason Crest

Mason Crest
450 Parkway Drive, Suite D
Broomall, PA 19008
www.masoncrest.com

Printed in the United States of America.

First printing
9 8 7 6 5 4 3 2 1

Series ISBN: 978-1-4222-2912-5
ISBN: 978-1-4222-2918-7
ebook ISBN: 978-1-4222-8908-2

The Library of Congress has cataloged the
hardcopy format(s) as follows:

Library of Congress Cataloging-in-Publication Data

Thompson, Helen, 1957-
  Managing employees / Helen Thompson.
      pages cm. – (Young adult library of small business and finance)
  Audience: Grade 7 to 8.
  ISBN 978-1-4222-2918-7 (hardcover) – ISBN 978-1-4222-2912-5 (series)
– ISBN 978-1-4222-8908-2 (ebook)
  1. Small business–Personnel management–Juvenile literature. 2. Supervision of employees–Juvenile literature. I. Title.
  HF5549.T484 2014
  658.3–dc23
                                    2013015651

Produced by Vestal Creative Services.
www.vestalcreative.com

CONTENTS

Introduction   6

1. What Does It Mean to Be a Leader?   11

2. Hiring Employees   19

3. Team Building   31

4. Delegating Responsibility   41

5. Managing Conflict   51

Find Out More   58

Vocabulary   59

Index   61

About the Author and Consultant   63

Picture Credits   64

INTRODUCTION

Brigitte Madrian, PhD

Small businesses serve a dual role in our economy. They are the bedrock of community life in the United States, providing goods and services that we rely on day in and day out. Restaurants, dry cleaners, car repair shops, plumbers, painters, landscapers, hair salons, dance studios, and veterinary clinics are only a few of the many different types of local small business that are part of our daily lives. Small businesses are also important contributors to the engines of economic growth and innovation. Many of the successful companies that we admire today started as small businesses run out of bedrooms and garages, including Microsoft, Apple, Dell, and Facebook, to name only a few. Moreover, the founders of these companies were all very young when they started their firms. Great business ideas can come from people of any age. If you have a great idea, perhaps you would like to start your own small business. If so, you may be wondering: What does it take to start a business? And how can I make my business succeed?

A successful small business rests first and foremost on a great idea—a product or service that other people or businesses want and are willing to pay for. But a good idea is not enough. Successful businesses start with a plan. A business plan defines what the business will do, who its customers will be, where the firm will be located, how the firm will market the company's product, who the firm will hire, how the business will be financed, and what, if any, are the firm's plans for future growth. If a firm needs a loan from a bank in order to start up, the bank will mostly likely want to see a written business plan. Writing a business plan helps an entrepreneur think

through all the possible road blocks that could keep a business from succeeding and can help convince a bank to make a loan to the firm.

Once a firm has the funding in place to open shop, the next challenge is to connect with the firm's potential customers. How will potential customers know that the company exists? And how will the firm convince these customers to purchase the company's product? In addition to finding customers, most successful businesses, even small ones, must also find employees. What types of employees should a firm hire? And how much should they be paid? How do you motivate employees to do their jobs well? And what do you do if employees don't get along? Managing employees is an important skill in running almost any successful small business.

Finally, firms must also understand the rules and regulations that govern how they operate their business. Some rules, like paying taxes, apply to all businesses. Other rules apply to only certain types of firms. Does the firm need a license to operate? Are there restrictions on where the firm can locate or when it can be open? What other regulations must the firm comply with?

Starting up a small business is a lot of work. But despite the hard work, most small business owners find their jobs

Managing Employees

rewarding. While many small business owners are happy to have their business stay small, some go on to grow their firms into more than they ever imagined, big companies that service customers throughout the world.

What will your small business do?

Brigitte Madrian, PhD
Aetna Professor of Public Policy and Corporate Management
Harvard Kennedy School

ONE

What Does It Mean to Be a Leader?

When you think of the word "leader," you might think of the president of the United States or the CEO (chief executive officer) of a big company. But anyone can be a leader—even you!

There are all sorts of leaders. Leaders can be in charge of governments, schools, businesses, and lots of other organizations. If you run your own business, you'll need to be a leader. Being a leader is especially important if you have employees. You will need to tell and show people what to do—but do it in a way that *motivates* people. Leaders make sure teams get things done!

Not all leaders are alike, but all good leaders possess qualities that inspire others to work together.

Leadership Skills

Good leaders have certain skills. Not everyone is born with leadership skills, but almost everyone can learn them over time. If you want to be a leader, you'll have to learn how to be one by actually doing it.

Everyone has a different style of leadership. But all leaders have similar goals. They all use their influence to get others to work together to accomplish a task—in other words, to get something done. The task might be getting a school project done, making laws in government, or raising money for a good cause.

To understand how leadership works, imagine you are working on a group school project. If you immediately start telling people which part of the project they have to do, without listening to anyone else, you're not showing very good leadership. You're taking charge, but you're not being a leader. In fact, the people in your group might not even listen to you at all because you haven't earned their respect. They'll just think you're bossy.

If you naturally take the lead, you could instead lead a **brainstorm** session with your group to come up with project ideas. This way you'll encourage people to come up with their own ideas and share them. Then you could help everyone else decide who will do which part and set a timeline for everyone to finish their parts. You're being a leader by encouraging others to finish the project, and organizing a way to make it happen. You're also leaving room for other people to be leaders too. Maybe someone else keeps in touch with the teacher and asks him whatever questions the group has. And someone else leads the writing part of the project and edits what everyone has written. Those people are being leaders too, just like you. They are just being leaders in a different way.

Good leaders are good at communicating. They can tell people what needs to be done and how to do it. However, good leaders don't just order people around. Instead, they encourage people to do tasks and show them the right way to do them. When you try to boss people around, you'll often find they push back; they don't always want to do what you tell them to do when you tell them to do it. When you listen to them, though, you can organize their ideas to make your project work.

ENTREPRENEURS

Entrepreneurs are a special type of business leader. Entrepreneurs take risks to make an idea work. People who start businesses, no matter how old they are, are entrepreneurs—because starting a business can be risky. You have to spend money to start a business. You have to spend a lot of time working on your business, rather than doing other things you like to do. You have to convince other people to buy what you're selling and help your business in other ways. As an entrepreneur's business grows, he or she will have to learn how to be a different sort of leader, to get people to work as a team to keep the business running.

No one can do everything by herself. Leaders need to know how to work with other people to get things done. They are good at working in teams. They don't just do all the work themselves. Instead, they figure out who will do which parts and divide up the responsibilities.

Another skill leaders have is decision-making. They need to be able to make decisions, often with help from other people. Leaders aren't uncomfortable about making decisions on the spot. They can't be wishy-washy, or nothing will ever get done.

Good leaders are also responsible. They aren't afraid to take on responsibility, and they do what they say they are going to do. They don't mind other people depending on them, and they get the job done, even if they have to ask for help from others.

Managing Employees

Leading in Business

People who start and run businesses are usually good leaders. They aren't afraid to make decisions or take responsibility. They are good at communicating with other people. For example, they are good at convincing customers to buy from their businesses, and they're good at working with employees. They work with others to make their businesses the best they can be.

KINDS OF LEADERS

Every leader is a little different, but there are some main categories. Ask yourself which category you fall under, and what your strengths and weaknesses are as that kind of leader.

- Inspirational. This kind of leader uses charm and personality to convince people to follow him. Inspirational leaders are good at listening and making other people feel comfortable and included in decision-making.
- Participative. These leaders direct a group of people who are focused on making a decision, and include the opinions of others before deciding.
- Directive. This leader tells others what to do and how to do it. Directive leaders often give out rewards and punishments for good and bad work.
- Leading-by-example. Generally, this leader does not tell people what to do but encourages them to take the right actions by showing them with her own actions.

Keeping your employees happy and productive is an important part of being a good leader.

Managing Employees

Business leadership is really important when it comes to employees. Not all businesses have employees, particularly those run by young people just starting out in the business world. But many businesses do have employees.

If you are the boss, you need to know how to be a good leader. You want happy and *productive* employees. Your business will grow if you know how to lead your employees well.

Learning how to be a good business leader takes time. You won't always know how to communicate with your employees. Sometimes, you won't give them enough room to do work on their own—and other times, you won't give them the guidance they need to get the job done. All leaders make mistakes sometimes. As a business owner, you'll have to figure it out along the way.

TWO

Hiring Employees

As your business grows, you may need an employee or two. You have a lot to do as a business owner, and you may need someone to help you do it.

But how do you even decide if you need an employee? And how do you go about hiring and managing them? You'll learn as you go, but you should also do some research ahead of time, so you know what you're getting yourself into and whether an employee is even right for your business. Employees help businesses grow—but they also can cost a lot of money.

Deciding to hire an employee can be a scary decision for a new business but needing to hire help is also a sign that your business is thriving!

Deciding to Hire

Deciding to hire an employee is a big decision. If you started a business alone, you'll have to get used to working with another person. You'll also have to get used to being a boss. Also, having employees can cost a lot of money.

You want to be sure that by hiring an employee, you will end up making more money than you'll be spending on your employee's **wages**. Think about it—you wouldn't want to hire an employee

Managing Employees

if you paid them $200 a week, but your employee didn't help you make any more money. You just lost the $200 a week for nothing.

The first sign you need an employee is when you realize you have too much to do. Let's say you run a traveling lemonade stand. You make lemonade and other drinks and then ride your bike around town with a lemonade stand attached, stopping wherever someone wants to buy from you. You're really busy in the summer, and you can't ever seem to hit every spot in town even though you could make more money if you could. You're getting tired from working so much, and you don't have enough time anymore to hang out with friends or get your summer project done for school. Maybe you need an employee to take over some of the work.

Before you dive in and get an employee, you should do some calculations and see if you can afford to hire someone. You consider buying another bike and lemonade stand on wheels. That would cost $400. You would also have to pay your employee, and you *estimate* you would pay them $9 an hour for 10 hours a week. You also think you could make $100 extra a week, based on how much people already buy.

You'll be spending $90 a week on wages, plus the new bike and stand. You'll be making $100 more a week. You decide that's not really worth it. You would only be making $10 extra a week, and it would take a long time to earn enough money to cover the cost of the new bike and stand. Plus, you don't have the extra money to spend on the bike and stand right now.

Then you think you could hire an employee to ride your own bike and stand, and you could work a little less. You would let them take over two whole days of selling. They work for $9 an hour for 12 hours a week, and make $150 extra a week. Spending $110 for $150, plus getting a rest from working seems like it's worth it. You decide to hire someone.

Hiring Employees

21

LAWS AND HIRING

Once you start thinking about hiring an employee, you'll have to pay attention to labor laws, which apply to bosses and employees. For example, you can't pay your employees less than minimum wage. The national government sets the minimum wage, but states can set their own higher minimum wages. Minimum wage changes every few years, so make sure you check with your state before you decide what to pay your employees. Child labor laws say you can't hire anyone under fourteen, and you can only make employees aged fifteen and sixteen work part time. If you want to hire young people, you'll have to keep those laws in mind. You also have to provide a safe workplace for your employees, or you could get in trouble with the law. In addition, you will have to pay more taxes once you hire an employee. Check out the Internal Revenue Service (IRS) for more details on employee taxes.

Advertising the Job

Now you have to get the word out that want to hire an employee. You can't assume an employee will magically land on your doorstep—you have to look for him or her.

You could advertise your job in the newspaper, online (like on the Craigslist site for your town or city), or put up posters around town. Spread the word that you're hiring to people you know too. A friend of a friend might be looking for a job.

When you advertise your job, decide what information you want to include in your advertisement. You should describe the

Managing Employees

job and what skills and tasks will be involved. You may also want to advertise how much you will be paying and how many hours a week the employee will be expected to work. The more you describe, the more likely you are to get good **applicants** to apply. You should advertise when the deadline is to apply, what applicants should include in their application, and how to send in their application. They can drop it off with you, mail it, or email it.

Many job applications ask people to include a résumé, which is a one-page overview of a person's experience and skills. People also often have to write a cover letter, which is an e-mail or letter introducing themselves and explaining why they would be a good fit for the job. Sometimes people include a list of contacts for references, people who will vouch for their experiences and qualifications. Decide what you want people to include in their application for your job.

Picking the Right Person

Hopefully you've gotten some interested **candidates** by now. You'll need to sort through everyone who has applied for the job you advertised, and pick the person you think will work best. You want someone who will work hard, gets along with you and other employees, and won't quit right away if the job wasn't what she expected.

First, take a look at the résumés people have sent you, if you asked for them. These will give you small snapshots of who people are and what experience they have. They definitely don't tell you everything about a person, though. Don't be too harsh when you're going over résumés. Just use this step to weed out candidates who don't seem like they would be a good fit at all. For example, if someone mentions in his application that he prefers

Letting people know about an open position at your business can mean putting out an ad in a newpaper or online, but it can also mean asking people you know if they know anyone well suited for the job.

Managing Employees

not to interact with people, don't interview him for a job selling lemonade!

Invite the people you choose as your top applicants to an interview. In an interview, you can talk to the person face-to-face. Have a list of questions handy so you remember what you want to ask. Good interview questions tell you a lot about the person you're interviewing.

In the interview, make sure the person you're talking to really wants the job you're offering. Maybe she is only applying because she needs some money and will take any job. The person who will work the hardest, though, will be the person who is really excited about the job. Ask candidates why they want the job and where they see themselves in a few years to get an idea of whether they are really excited about the job or not.

Besides an interview, you may want to have the top candidates actually work with you for a couple hours. By asking them to do a small job, you can see exactly how they work and if they will get along with you and any other employees you have. If they seem like they hate the work, or they don't seem to be paying attention while working, don't hire them.

Pay attention to what candidates do outside the interview too. Notice how they interact with other people besides you. They should be polite and respectful to others, no matter who they are. Of course, they will be polite to you, because you're interviewing them, but they should also be polite to your family if you happen to be interviewing them at home, polite to customers, and polite to anyone else who may be around. Watching what they do in and out of the interview will give you a better idea of what they will be like once they start working.

Hiring Employees 25

Interviewing potential employees isn't only about finding out who is best qualified for a job but also judging who will be the best fit for your business.

Managing Employees

INTERVIEW QUESTIONS TO CONSIDER

Make sure you ask good questions when you interview job applicants, so you figure out who will make a good employee. Here are some examples of questions you might want to ask:

- What's the one accomplishment you're most proud of? Why?
- What are your strengths and weaknesses?
- Why do you want this job?
- What can you bring to this job that other candidates can't?
- How do you keep yourself organized?
- Why should I hire you?
- Do you have any questions for me?

Also, by law, you cannot ask questions about a person's race, age, religion, sexual orientation, or whether or not he or she is married.

Picking an Employee

Now that you've interviewed a bunch of people, you have to choose the one to hire. You don't really have one right or wrong answer. Several people might work well with your business. You just have to pick the best one!

Write down the candidates' answers to interview questions and any notes you have about them, so you remember who all the candidates are. When you get to the end of your interviews, think about who will be best.

Don't just pick a friend who applied, or the person you think you have the most in common with. Even if you end up finding out that you and an applicant have the same favorite movie, he might not be the best person for the job.

You do want to get along with the person you hire. If you felt good about the conversation you had with an applicant during an interview, and she is **qualified** for the job, you may have found the person you're going to hire.

Once you decide, you have to tell the person you want to hire. Try not to make him wait too long, or he might get another job instead. At this point, your choice might even decide not to work for you. If that happens, go over the people you interviewed and pick your second choice.

If your first choice says yes, you have a new employee! Meet with him again and discuss everything to make sure he knows what's going on. Have him fill out the legal paperwork (again, check out the IRS website), and figure out when he'll start working.

Real Life Business

Robbie Kelly is one young person who knows what it's like to run a busy company. He started a landscaping business at the age of nine, and he has been running it ever since.

Over the last few years, he has gotten so many customers that he has had to hire employees to work with them all. One of his first employees was his younger brother, Willie. Willie is the **sales manager**, who creates posters to put around town. Robbie is still involved with advertising, though. "He makes them, I approve them," Robbie says.

Robbie has hired other employees as well as his brother. He hires local young people who want landscaping jobs. Willie helps

Managing Employees

him keep track of other employees and make sure they're doing their job.

Together, they figure out how much to pay them, hire new employees, and even fire employees who don't work out. Robbie explains, "Mainly I am looking for kids who can take hard, physical work."

Robbie sets a good example of the work he wants done, working long hours in sun, rain, and snow. He has shown he's a good leader, by setting an example and by managing his employees well.

Everyone brings something unique and important to a team. Team building helps everyone work together.

Managing Employees

exercises help make people comfortable with each other; they help make everyone into a team, not just a bunch of individual people who all happen to work together.

Team building involves taking time out of the regular workday to focus on becoming a team. Employees (and often bosses) do special activities together that help them get to know each other and learn how to interact with each other.

Team building has several goals. It helps people who work together communicate and cooperate better. Team building can get employees motivated to get work done and help the business grow. It helps people trust each other. In the end, team building makes businesses better and helps them grow and make more money.

Some Good Exercises

Team building comes in lots of forms. You might already have participated in some team-building activities yourself, if you have ever been to a summer camp or even on your first day of a new school year. If you've ever played name games, cooperation games, or trust games, you've done a team-building exercise.

Chances are, your employees aren't really going to want to practice trust falls with each other. You have plenty of options for more *professional* team-building exercises, which are more appropriate for work and will help people become a team.

You could all take a field trip together. You could go somewhere that has to do with your business, or choose somewhere that is just plain fun. Go to the movies, head to a restaurant, or cook dinner together. Having field trips outside work helps people get to know each other without feeling uncomfortable interacting at work.

DOES YOUR BUSINESS NEED TEAM BUILDING?

Some businesses struggle more than others to encourage employees to work together and get things done. If your business shows any of these signs, it might be time for a team-building day.

- Lots of conflicts or fights between employees, or yourself and an employee.
- A lot of miscommunication or misunderstandings between employees, or yourself and employees.
- Lack of motivation, or your employees are not working hard.
- Customer complaints about how they are being served or complaints abut working with certain employees.
- Decisions are made that don't end up turning into actions.
- Several new employees who do not feel like they are part of the business yet.

You can also have you and all your employees get together to volunteer. Serve food at a local food pantry. Build a home for Habitat for Humanity. Clean up trash for an environmental day. Working together to make the world a better place will definitely bring your work team closer together. Search around for local **non-profits** that take volunteers, and then have your employees help you decide where to volunteer.

Managing Employees

A third team-building choice is doing a **_professional development_** activity. Help people learn more about their job and help them do even better work by giving them unusual activities to do. Go see a speaker giving a talk on working in a team. Attend a class together about advertising online. Go to a conference, where everyone can choose classes that will teach them a little about the job they do.

No matter what you choose, team building should make people interact with each other. As people get more comfortable interacting with each other in a setting outside normal work, they'll be more comfortable interacting at work too.

Making Team-Building a Part of Your Business

All this stuff sounds great, but you have to make it an actual part of your business. Team building can take a lot of time and effort, but it will pay off!

Going back to our traveling lemonade stand example, suppose you have decided to hire three new employees because your business is doing so well. They don't really know each other, though, because they are all off riding their own bikes and stands. When they do have to interact, they are awkward and don't really know how to get things done together. For example, you asked two of them to work together at a big festival in your town, but they ended up in a fight. One of your employees is also pretty lazy, and she doesn't seem excited about the job.

Having some fun with your team might seem like a distraction but taking some time to get your team motivated and excited can really pay off!

Managing Employees

TEAM—BUILDING GAMES

If you do want to use some camp-style games to get your employees working as a team, here are a few suggestions:

- Mine Field: Objects are scattered randomly in a space. One person is blindfolded while another person guides them with words through the "mine field." This game works on communication skills.
- Best Moments: Everyone shares the best moment in their life, which helps everyone get to know each other.
- Sales Challenge: Each person gets an everyday object she has to write an advertisement for or otherwise convince the rest of the group to buy.
- What I Bring to the Team: Everyone reflects on why he was hired, and tells one or two things he is good at and one or two things he needs to improve.

You decide you all need to do some team-building exercises. You want everyone to get along, and you want everyone to be able to communicate better. You also want all your employees to be excited about their jobs and work hard.

You can't afford to take a whole day off for team building, but you give everyone a half-day off to get together for a picnic at the beach on the local lake. Everyone has to bring something to eat, so you all have to communicate ahead of time about what you're bringing. One person brings hot dogs and buns, another brings salad, another drinks, and you bring the dessert. Right away, you have worked together to make the picnic happen.

Team building improves relationships between employees and can increase the speed and quality of the work they do together.

Managing Employees

At the picnic, you all get to know each other a little better. You don't talk about work. Instead, you talk about your friends and family, and what you like to do in your free time. The two employees who were mad at each other find out they both love soccer. One even brought a soccer ball, so they start kicking the ball around. You suspect they'll get along better now that they know they have something in common.

After the picnic, you feel like you know your employees better. You know a little more about how to talk to each of them and how to motivate them. And your employees seem pretty happy. They are all talking to each other and seem excited for the next week at work. Your team-building picnic won't solve every employee problem you'll ever have, but it looks like it might have started to make everyone into a team.

FOUR

Delegating Responsibility

If you're hiring employees, you've realized that you can't run your business by yourself. Not being able to handle everything yourself doesn't mean you've failed. In fact, it means just the opposite in business terms! Your business is so successful and has grown so much that you need help handling all the customers you have.

Who Does What?

Delegating responsibility means figuring out who does what in a business. You can't do it all, so you have to figure out the best people for each job.

Being a good leader means knowing who, of your employees, is best suited for handling a task or responsibility.

Managing Employees

In the lemonade stand example, you now have three employees, plus yourself, doing work. You obviously hired them because there was just too much work for you to do by yourself. But who should do what? You can't hire just anyone for any job.

First, there are the tasks that everyone has to do because it's why you hired them. Everyone has to bike around town and sell lemonade from the mobile stand. They have to talk to customers and get them to buy lemonade.

But maybe one of your employees isn't as good at selling lemonade as the other two. The first two employees you hired love riding around and working with customers. The third one doesn't like biking very far, and she doesn't always like interacting with customers. Instead, that employee really likes working with numbers and keeping track of the money the business makes. She has actually given you a couple really good suggestions about *finances* that have saved you some money.

As the boss, you can decide to let that employee take over some of your financial duties. She can sell lemonade part of the time, and keep track of money part of the time. You don't really like the whole finance part anyway, so you're also doing yourself a favor. You still want to know what's going on with the finances, and you meet with your employee every week to find out what she did with the money that week. You have successfully *delegated* responsibility.

Making Responsible Choices

As the person who delegates the work, you have to know who is good at what. You don't want to assign someone who hates *customer service* the job of talking to people door-to-door about your business. He won't like the task, and he probably won't do a very good job.

Delegating Responsibility

43

Hiring capable employees in the first place will save you much of the headache of delegating responsibilities.

Managing Employees

The first step in making good choices about who should do what is to hire the right people. If you pick people who are good at the jobs you hire them to do, delegating responsibility doesn't have to be so hard.

But first you do have to decide what kinds of jobs you need to hire people for. Do you need more advertising? Maybe you should hire someone who only works on advertising. Or maybe you think you should be working behind the scenes, while someone else does the selling and working with customers. What you decide to stop doing depends on what you like and don't like to do, and what your business needs.

At some point, you might not even be the best person to do some of the jobs required in your business. When you first start a business, you are the one who knows what's going on and what you want the business to look like. You learn how to run it along the way.

Eventually, if your business is successful, you'll start needing some *expertise*. You might not know how to do your taxes, so you could hire an accountant. You don't know how to write a good *grant* application to get money, so you hire someone to write grants for you. Depending on what you need, having other people do some work will free you up to focus on what you know and are good at.

How to Delegate

Once you decide what responsibilities you're delegating and who you're delegating them to, you have to do it! Delegating can be hard if you still want to be in control of everything in your business.

Meeting regularly is a good way to remain aware of your employees' progress and keep up their morale.

Managing Employees

You should give your employees enough independence to do their jobs. If you're not used to other people maintaining your website, for example, you might want to watch what they're doing all the time and give them pointers. That's okay to do at first, when you're telling your employees how to maintain the website, but after that, you're just being bossy. You delegated responsibilities so you could have more time to do other things. If you're still hanging on to old tasks by watching employees do them, you haven't saved yourself any time.

You need to trust your employees to do their jobs. They might mess up once in a while, but they'll get better as they learn their tasks. Learn how to be okay with mistakes once in a while—you'll make them too. Give your employees enough training and support that they'll know how to fix mistakes.

Even though you shouldn't be hovering over other people's work, you should still keep an eye on what they're doing. You're still the boss, after all. You want to give your employees directions without telling them what to do all the time. Most people work best and hardest when they know what they're expected to do but are free to do it how they want.

Think of it this way: You're guiding the big picture while other people take care of details. You decide how you're going to sell your product or services. You decide if advertisements are good enough to post. Your employees might do the actual selling, and designing and posting of the ads.

Hold a meeting once a week or once every other week to check-in on how everyone is doing. Go over what they've all done for the week, and if they have any questions or need a new project. You might even hold meetings with each employee independently every few weeks.

Delegating Responsibility

STARTING A BUSINESS STEP BY STEP

Starting a business can be a lot of work, but it's exciting and rewarding work! Here are a few steps to starting up a serious business.

1. Decide on your business. Ask yourself what you're good at and what you enjoy doing. Can you make your interests into a business that makes you money?
2. Research your competition. Figure out if other businesses are already selling what you want to sell and if there's room for another similar business. Take a look at what similar businesses are charging their customers to figure out your own prices.
3. Name your business. Pick a name that is creative but still tells people what your business does.
4. Create a business plan. Business plans are basically roadmaps for success—they cover what your business will be and how you will run it.
5. Make a list of your expenses. What are the things you need to buy to start your business? Will you need materials, space, employees, or training?
6. Find money. You'll need money to cover all your expenses. You can spend your own money, or find people who are willing to give you a loan.
7. Advertise. Print out flyers, advertise in the newspaper, and use the Internet to spread the word about your business. Make sure your ads have enough information, including what you sell, how

Managing Employees

much it is, and how to contact you. Get business cards and hand them out to people you meet.

8. Keep track of finances. Write down all the money you spend and the money you make. That way, you'll be able to see if you're making money.

9. Pay taxes. If you make enough money, you legally have to pay taxes. Check with the IRS (Internal Revenue Service) to figure out if you made enough to pay taxes.

10. Decide if you need to hire employees after your business is up and running. If you do, take steps to hire employees who will work hard and add value to your business.

Imagine you're sick for a few days. What would happen at your company? Would it fall apart because no one knows what they should be doing without you? You don't want that to happen! Employees should be independent enough that they feel good working without you for a little while. But you should plan on guiding the whole business and make big decisions.

Once you figure out how to delegate responsibilities, your business will run better than ever! You should have more time to do work or even take some time off, and your employees will be helping your business grow.

Delegating Responsibility

FIVE

Managing Conflict

When you run a business alone, you don't really have to worry about getting along with yourself. As soon as you hire employees, you do have to worry how everyone will interact. You might hire an employee with whom you don't get along. Or you might hire two employees who just can't seem to work together.

To make your business a good place to work, you'll have to learn how to deal with employee conflict. Good bosses and good leaders can manage conflict and keep work going smoothly.

Dealing with Conflict

Conflict is what happens when people disagree about something, and it causes *tension*. Conflicts could be arguments. Ignoring someone or disrespecting him is a form of conflict. Talking about people behind their backs is conflict.

The very first step to dealing with conflict is noticing it's there. Some people just like to ignore conflict and hope it will go away. You won't get very far as a boss if you ignore conflict. Ignoring conflict doesn't mean it's not there. Conflicts get worse and worse the longer they last. Dealing with them right away is the best idea.

Imagine the two employees at your mobile lemonade stand business still aren't getting along, even though they seemed to be doing better after the team-building picnic. One of them comes to work late almost every day. You're kind of annoyed at him, and you have spoken to him once or twice about coming to work on time. Your other employee is always on time and gets annoyed when her coworker is late. The other day, they were supposed to work together again at a big event. Predictably, the first employee was late. The second employee ended up yelling at him and made the whole day very tense

When you see both of them the next day, you can tell something is wrong. They aren't speaking to each other, and they both look really angry. You consider just ignoring the whole thing, because you don't want to deal with them again. But you ask what's wrong, because you don't want them to explode at each other later on.

As soon as you know something is wrong, act. Get the people in the conflict to meet with you and find out what is going on from both points of view. You can decide whether to meet with them separately or together. If they're really angry at each other, it might be best to talk to them individually. If you think they can handle being in the same room, talk to them together so they can start to understand the other person's point of view too.

Managing Employees

In the lemonade stand situation, you decide to talk to the two employees together because it's almost the end of the workday. You ask that each of them let the other speak without interrupting and listen to what the other person has to say. The employee who is always on time explains what happened yesterday, and you feel yourself getting a little angry at the late employee. Then the late employee gets a chance to talk.

He says he is always late because he has to take care of his little brother when his mom isn't home. His family can't afford to send his little brother to an after-school program or hire a babysitter. Your employee has to watch him until his mom comes home. He doesn't mind taking care of his brother, but it means he is sometimes late to work.

REASONS FOR CONFLICT

People come into conflict with each other for all sorts of reasons. At work, people often feel like they're competing with each other. If one person is selling more, or making a better impression on the boss, other people might feel bad. Stress causes conflicts too, because people have less patience when they're under deadlines or have a lot to do all at once. If a business is going through a big change, like hiring more employees or changing the way they sell things, employees may not be able to handle the change all at once. Conflicts end up happening as employees figure out how to deal with the change. Other conflicts happen because employees just don't get along and have really different personalities.

Managing Conflict

You and the other employee didn't know that. You're glad you took the time to listen, because you can tell the employee isn't just being lazy or irresponsible. You can already see that the other employee is less angry now that she sees he isn't being lazy. Now you can figure out how to work it out.

The next step is to figure out how to solve the problem in front of you. You should find a way to make the conflict less tense, so that your employees can keep on working together right away. Even just having your employees hear each other's point of view will help get rid of some of the tension from the conflict.

When you're deciding what to do, make sure to look at the conflict from all sides. If you favor one employee unfairly, you'll just add to the conflict, rather than get rid of it. And let your employees have a say in what happens. When they feel like they're a part of the decision, they're more likely to be happy with the decision.

Finally, figure out how to handle the reason the conflict happened in the first place. If you just solve conflicts as they happen, you risk having the same conflict happen over and over again. You can only move on by really getting at what is happening.

In the case, your employee is always late because he has to take care of his little brother. You can't change that, but you can change how you deal with your employee. You decide to schedule him for later in the day and on weekends when he doesn't have to take care of his brother. You even give him a couple hours of work from home every week, working on the website. That way, he can continue to work 10 hours a week, but he has a little more choice about when he works.

You ask if that plan is okay with your other employee. She's a little worried she'll have to do more work to make up for her co-worker. You see her point and tell her you'll rearrange everyone's

Managing Employees

schedule a little so no one has to do an unfair amount of work. You'll have to tell your third employee, so it doesn't come as a surprise when his schedule changes a little. You and your employees agree to check in again in two weeks to see if everything is working out. If the late employee does his work at home and stops being late, you know you solved the problem!

Not Always Bad

Conflicts will happen. When people work together, you can count on someone disagreeing at some point. Conflict is totally fine. It can make people think about what they believe and how they do things. In the end, the way conflicts are **resolved** might make work better for everyone and even make the business stronger.

Maybe your two employees will continue to disagree about things, but sometimes it works out for the best. For example, they disagree about the best route to take selling lemonade. They come into conflict with each other because they both have different ideas. But they can talk about their ideas, and they realize they can combine bits of each route to come up with the best way to bike around town. Because they had different ideas and could talk about their conflict, they came up with a **compromise** that will sell more lemonade and grow the business.

However, you and your employees can't let conflicts get out of hand. When disagreements make people too uncomfortable to come to work or end up in shouting matches, conflicts have gone too far. Now they are hurtful instead of productive.

Managing conflict doesn't mean avoiding any conflict it all. It does mean avoiding having an employee storm out of the office or quit because he can't get along with other people.

When you learn to manage conflict, you'll have a happier and more productive workplace. No one wants to work in a place that's tense all the time. As the boss, you are responsible for making sure conflicts are managed well.

Managing Employees as a Young Person

When people imagine a boss at work, they usually picture someone who is older. But bosses can be young people too. If you have your own business, you may be a boss yourself soon. But being a young boss could also lead to conflicts with employees who might be older than you. They may not want to take direction from someone who is younger.

A young entrepreneur named Sean Belnick knows what it's like to be a young boss. He started an online office furniture company when he was fourteen. At first, he was working by himself, but his business grew quickly and he began to hire employees. In 2011, he had seventy-five employees to help him.

Luckily for Sean, he has found that being a young boss has worked out well. He says, "I think most employees think that it is 'cool' to have a young boss. We have a more relaxed work environment and it is not as stressful. Employees are also less intimidated with a younger boss and are more likely to come to me with ideas and their true feelings, which ultimately help the company." Sean sees his age as a good thing, not something that adds to conflicts.

Being a good business leader and managing employees well pays off in a big way. Once you make the decision to hire employees, like Robbie and Sean did, you'll need to learn a whole new set of skills. Employee-management skills are good to have, because your business will run better. You'll be able to take those skills wherever you go in your future, too. You'll be the best businessperson you can be!

Find Out More

ONLINE

Internal Revenue Services (IRS)
www.irs.gov

The Leader in Me: The 7 Habits of Happy Kids
www.theleaderinme.org/the-7-habits-for-kids

Tips on Hiring New Employees for Your Small Business
www.businessbewareshow.com/2012/01/13/tips-hiring-employees

Young Entrepreneurs
www.entrepreneur.com/tsu/index.html

IN BOOKS

Bernstein, Daryl. *Better Than a Lemonade Stand! Small Business Ideas for Kids*. New York: Aladdin, 2012.

Drew, Naomi. *The Kids' Guide to Working Out Conflicts*. Minneapolis, Minn.: Free Spirit Publishing, 2004.

Karnes, Frances and Suzanne Bean. *Leadership for Students*. Waco, Tex.: Prufrock Press, 2010.

Mariotti, Steve. *The Young Entrepreneur's Guide to Starting and Running a Business*. New York: Three Rivers Press, 2000.

Vocabulary

Applicants: people who are applying for something.

Brainstorm: a group discussion used to produce new ideas.

Candidates: people who will potentially be hired for a job.

Compromise: an agreement in which each side gives up something.

Customer service: interactions with the people who are buying things from a business.

Delegated: gave a job to someone else.

Estimate: guess, make a projection.

Expertise: skill or knowledge of a particular task or subject.

Finances: the way in which money is handled and kept track of in a business.

Grant: money given by a government or other organization to another organization for a specific purpose.

Inspire: fill someone with the urge or ability to do something.

Motivates: makes someone interested and enthusiastic about doing something.

Non-profits: organizations who make money in order to achieve a social goal, not to give money to those who own the organization.

Productive: able to do a lot of work.

Professional: serious and acting in a mature way that's appropriate for a paid job.

Professional development: skills and knowledge learned to get better at a job.

Qualified: capable of and having the right skills for doing a task.

Resolved: settled, explained, or answered.

Sales manager: person who directs how a product or service is advertised and distributed to customers.

Tension: strain or stress between people.

Wages: money earned on a job.

Index

advertising 28, 35, 45
applicants 23, 25, 27
arguments 51

Belnick, Sean 56
boss 13, 17, 20, 31, 43, 47,
    52–53, 56

Chief Executive Officer
    (CEO) 11
communication 37
compromise 55, 59
cooperation 33
conflicts 34, 51–56, 58
customers 7–9, 15, 25, 28,
    41, 43, 45, 48

decisions 14–15, 34, 49

entrepreneurs 14

finances 43, 49

games 33, 37

hiring 19–20, 22, 41, 44, 53

interviews 27

Kelly, Robbie 28

laws 13, 22
leaders 11–15, 17, 51
listening 13, 15

responsibility 5, 14–15, 41–
    43, 45

sales 28, 37

taxes 8, 22, 45, 49

team building 5, 31–35, 37–38

teams 11, 14

wages 20–22, 60

About the Author and Consultant

Helen Thompson lives in upstate New York. She worked first as a social worker and then became a teacher as her second career.

Brigitte Madrian is the Aetna Professor of Public Policy and Corporate Management at the Harvard Kennedy School. Before coming to Harvard in 2006, she was on the faculty at the University of Pennsylvania Wharton School (2003–2006), the University of Chicago Graduate School of Business (1995–2003) and the Harvard University Economics Department (1993–1995). She is also a research associate and co-director of the Household Finance working group at the National Bureau of Economic Research. Dr. Madrian received her PhD in economics from the Massachusetts Institute of Technology and studied economics as an undergraduate at Brigham Young University. She is the recipient of the National Academy of Social Insurance Dissertation Prize (first place, 1994) and a two-time recipient of the TIAA-CREF Paul A. Samuelson Award for Scholarly Research on Lifelong Financial Security (2002 and 2011).

Picture Credits